CW00794770

BRITISH COUNCIL | **75** YEARS OF CULTURAL RELATIONS

BRITISH PAVILION
VENICE BIENNALE 2009

STEVE M^CQUEEN

GIARDINI

NOTEBOOK

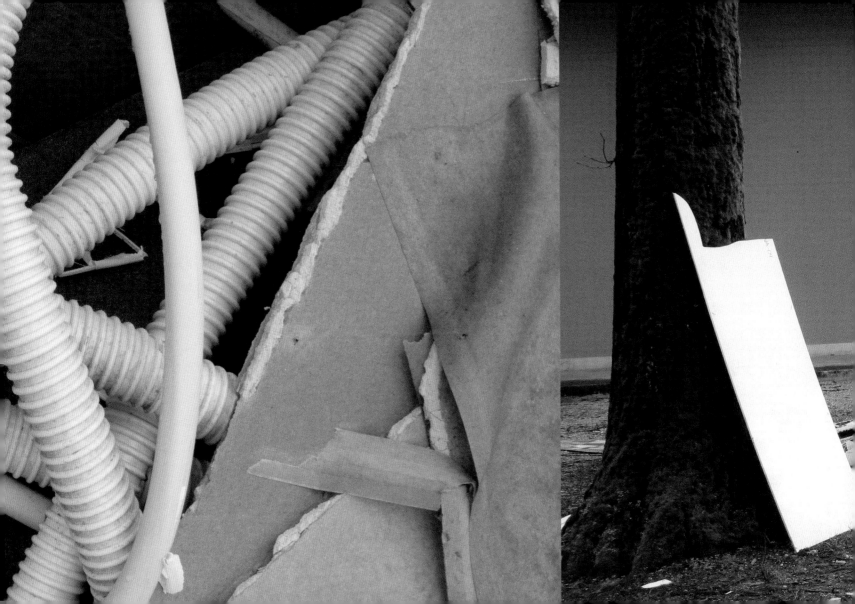

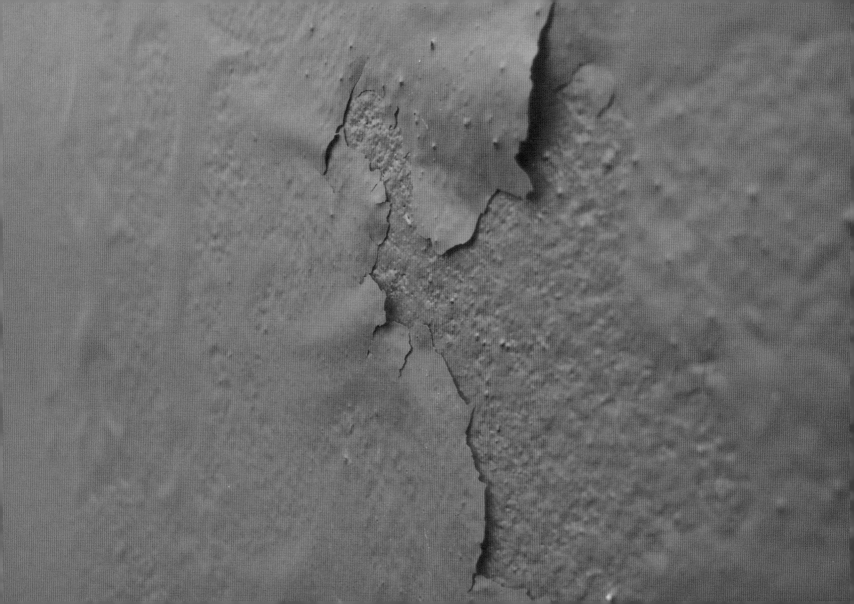

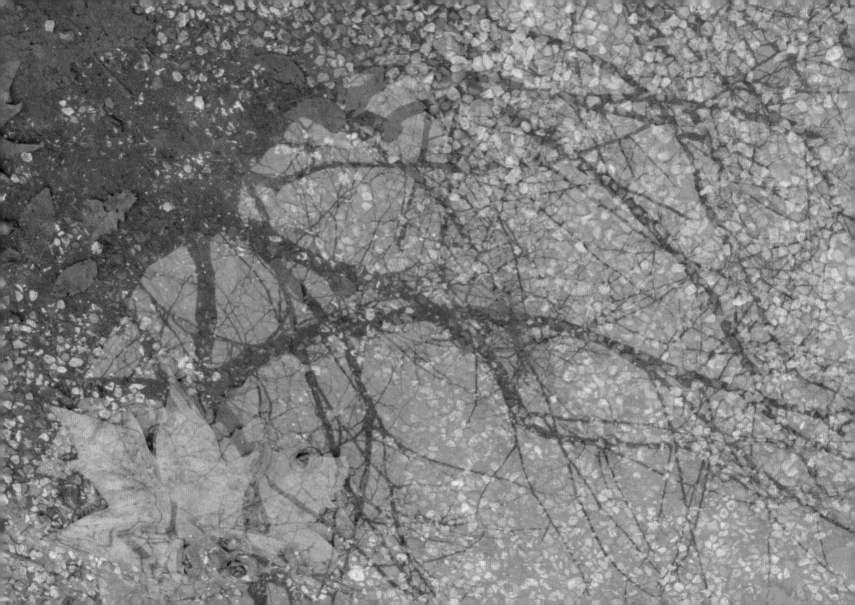

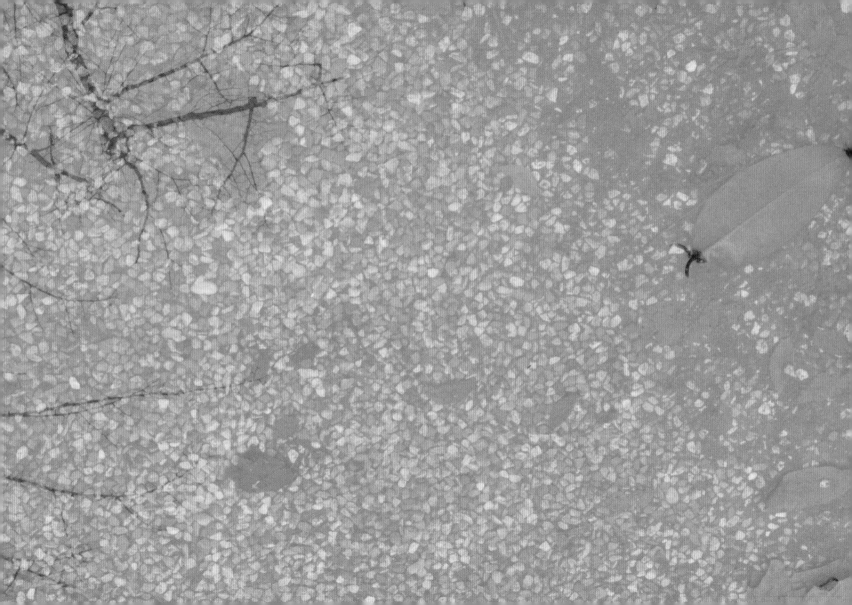

Giardini: A Fairytale

T.J. Demos

A visually sumptuous film of thirty minutes, *Giardini* comprises two projections set side-by-side, which steadily gather a series of evocative vignettes. Rainwater splashes out a quickening rhythm on the hard surfaces of grey and black stones; the blurred shapes of dogs move about restlessly, as if searching for food amid heaps of refuse on an otherwise grand promenade; dark silhouettes of an orderly row of trees create abstract patterns against a blue crepuscular sky; a young man, seemingly anxious, with darting eyes, smokes in the shadows. With alternating bluish-black and warm reddish tones, powerfully and suggestively imagistic, this film radiates a magical aura, one teeming with possibility rather than defined by a single narrative or by the clarity and authority of documentary information.

Like McQueen's past films, such as *Caribs' Leap/Western Deep* (2002) and *Gravesend* (2007), *Giardini* denies clear links between representation and significance, between form and content – not to exclude reference but instead to allow the image's potential meanings to crystallise, its facets reflecting numerous paths of fabulation. Indeed, the film's suspension of its images in a field of multiple possibilities defines its power: to release life from belonging to any certain code, clear narrative, or restrictive regimen, and to do so in the quintessential location of national order: the Giardini of the Venice Biennale. As its title indicates, the film is set in the famous exhibition grounds, the location of the ageing national pavilions – the American, Italian, Swiss, and Israeli are among those shown. These otherwise well-known monuments are shown here in an unexpected light, during the interim between biennales, in the down-time and during the nights, in the shadows of spectacle. The renowned gardens are thereby recast as a site where everything is suddenly up for grabs, seems unfamiliar and unpredictable, where life is shown to assume forms of creative survival that transcend the fanfare of the great exhibition. Few visitors, if any, experience it as such. In this sense, the film is only conveniently attached to Venice's Giardini, and indeed its grounds are transported elsewhere.

With great subtlety, the film's vignettes nevertheless sketch several plotlines, avoiding a non-signifying abstraction. Consider, first, the dogs, their unfocused shapes gradually sharpening into legible figures, which wander about the empty buildings and walkways throughout the film, as if in some post-apocalyptic near-future. Strikingly, they appear to be greyhounds, scrounging in the rubbish, animals who have outlived their value to the races are now abandoned to their own devices. These are dogs that should be dead, like the retired racehorse in the artist's *Running Thunder* (2007), a film that meditates on the tragic extermination of animal life when it is cruelly deemed useless to sport. In light of these canine scavengers, it is hard not to think of the Biennale as similarly outmoded, feeding on its own obsolete national traditions as a means of continued existence. Forming another potential tale, the film portrays an anonymous young black man waiting in the Giardini at night, alone, as if expectantly. He seems shifty, unpredictable, incongruous in this setting, closer in appearance to a hard-up immigrant than a smartly-dressed cultural tourist, even though there is no way of gauging his identity one way or another. If stateless, then the film locates him in the shadows of national grandeur and imperial display, as the interloper – a refugee? an asylum seeker? – temporarily inhabits nationalism's majestic court, undermining its power and legitimacy. Immediately following these shots, another sequence forces a reconsideration: two figures in the dark middle-ground at night approach one another and engage in an extended intimate embrace. Pointing less to a love affair and more to the anonymity of cruising or prostitution, the connection is ultimately shrouded in ambiguity, for there is no indication of who of these figures are, or of the outcome of their amorous entwinement.

These stories are finely sketched, hinted at without grounding or substance, exemplifying the film's light touch. Its extraordinary finesse evokes multiple potential tales without authorising them with contextual information. There is no voice-over or subtitles. If the film offers no narrative allegory or clear moral, neither is it a documentary exposé of the "truth" of the Giardini – its social, environmental, ecological reality – outside of the Biennale's activities. We know that greyhounds, for instance, do not in fact prowl these gardens (rather the area is known for its feral cats). *Giardini*, then, constructs a fictional world and does so with great care, although its stories are not necessarily impossible accounts of what might actually happen. This fiction, which exists within the realm of the possible, displaces another fiction, an exhibition that brings the Giardini to life every year (with the alternating art and architecture biennales) by engaging the signs of empire set within its midst: the national grandeur of the pavilions, many built during Italy's fascist 1930s, after the marshland was drained by Napoleon's engineers following the French invasion in 1797. It is on these grounds redolent of imperial pageantry, where nations have proclaimed their splendour via architectural and artistic presentations for more than a century, that McQueen's film is premiered.

Spinning a fiction of multiple strands, *Giardini* advances what author Jorge Luis Borges termed "a garden of forking paths" in a well-known story from his book *Labyrinths*. Referenced by Gilles Deleuze in *Cinema 2: The Time Image*, it serves for him as a metaphor for the cinematic crystallisation of time, for its winding of the real and the virtual into a knot of indeterminate relation, for the co-existence of multiple potential narrative threads that characterises post-WWII-era film, from Alain Resnais to Federico Fellini.[1] For the film's positioning of geography as a site of creative potential – where different forms of life beyond conventional regimes that structure existence become possible – mirrors the re-invention of film as a locus of generative imagination. *Giardini* not only disarticulates expectations about a charged landscape, but opens up new forms of cinematic perception, which occurs in several ways, defining the film's singularity.

First, *Giardini*'s split-screen format disavows the definitive account, the singular expression, its doubled image announcing contingency, multiplicity, potentiality. Our gaze is consequently trained on the out-of-frame, defining a second aspect of perceptual shift: not only is this fact indicated by the dual screens – any one image is necessarily incomplete, supplemental, and therefore the gaps between and within the images become operative as dark forces of virtuality – but also the camera emphasises its blurred focus, extreme close-ups and tightly framed compositions of peripheral areas, and nocturnal and shadowy scenes. In this regard, McQueen's filmic concentration

---

1. Gilles Deleuze, *Cinema 2: The Time-Image*, trans. Hugh Tomlinson and Robert Galeta (Minneapolis: University of Minnesota Press, 1989), see pp. 49ff.

on the out-of-frame (*le hors champ*) mirrors the displaced portrayal of Venice's gardens in winter as a place of outsiders and interlopers, joining the immigrant and the illicit, as opposed to the front and centre, the belonging and appropriate during the exhibition's limelight. As well, chiming church bells and a cheering crowd – a manifestation? a protest? a football game? – are heard, not seen, as the soundtrack redoubles this logic of looking awry. We remain in the shadows, focused on the realm of the un-belonging, the non-participatory. Then, there is the imaging of forms and shapes prior to representation. The film presents a mosaic of colours, lights and movements, as perception is made to precede language's reference and signification; the perceived exists beyond comprehension, outside a reliable knowledge base. Finally, the film's sense of time locates us within a temporality that suspends narrative's developmental order (one thinks of cinematic precedents in the work of Jean-Luc Godard and Chantal Akerman). Shots during day and night cycle back and forth, unpredictably, breaking the sense of natural chronology. As well, the frequent experience of slow-paced footage blurs the real time of life, of watching, with the virtual inner-time of cinema, defying the timelessness of empire. Image and sound, now and then, here and there, become de-linked, resembling the way that Deleuze describes the time-image, with the effect that habitual modes of looking are challenged and creatively reinvented.

As *Giardini* is distinguished by its anti-spectacular, innovative portrayal of a symbolically charged environment, one might be tempted to see in it the traces of McQueen's earlier works, such as *Drumroll* (1998), in which he recorded a New York city street by using cameras secured within a revolving metal oil drum, or *Exodus* (1992/97), an evocative short film of two black men carrying palm trees down a London street, which locates the diasporic in Britain's post-colonial capital. These past films construct a realm of the senses – visual, haptic, aural – similarly situated beyond narrative legibility and metaphorical obviousness. Yet that's not to say that *Giardini* entails a disengagement from the political concerns of the artist's more recent films, and indeed McQueen observes that *Giardini* is as political as his other works which address post-colonial contexts and the history and continuation of violent oppression.[2] These include *Caribs' Leap/ Western Deep*, which depict migrant workers performing back-breaking labour in a South African gold mine, juxtaposed with shots of Grenada, eliciting the seventeenth-century historical event when a group of Caribs threw themselves from a cliff rather than surrender to the invading French army; *Gravesend*, a film that portrays miners in the Congolese jungle digging for coltan, a valuable mineral processed in European electronics labs shown in subsequent shots, thereby connecting the state of violent lawlessness with the neo-colonial demand for its natural resources; and *Hunger* (2008), McQueen's celebrated feature release that dramatises the last six weeks of the life of Bobby

---

2. As the artist explained to me in Amsterdam on 20 April, 2009.

Sands, leader of the 1981 IRA hunger strike who famously died in Belfast's HM Maze prison.[3]

In these past films, quasi-documentary footage of physical abjection – of manual labour and imprisonment – draw colonial and neo-colonial contexts together into a single historical trajectory of imperialism, of economic and political inequality. But simultaneously, McQueen's depictions reject the simple exposure of a definitive and authoritatively informed account of reality. Doing so avoids the reinforcement of oppression in representation deemed transparent, as if its reality were an unavoidable truth or an ontological reality. Yet this complex position does not entail a plea for escapism, but rather a double negation that opens up different forms of political empowerment than the ones associated with conventional documentary practice, based on a presumed neutrality and objectivity in approaching the seemingly transparent meaning of reality. The artist's films equally eschew the political instrumentalization of art, which forfeits aesthetic complexity in favour of activist mobilisation, the aesthetics of cinematic affect for straightforward information.

Avoiding these traps, McQueen defines a seemingly impossible stance – which makes his films all the more compelling for their eliciting the unavoidable paradoxes of life: to bring the existence of injustice to visibility, and to reveal the system of oppression as contingent, and therefore contestable. His films craft a moving perceptual space, in other words, that rejects the totality of control, even as the film glimpses it. Miners are shown as luminous bodies within their hellish prisons; the prisoner Sands undergoes an act of impossible transcendence in his bodily dematerialisation, taking political control of his life by dying, which is the tragedy – and also dark victory – on which the film unapologetically turns.

Giardini continues the political commitment of McQueen's cinema in two ways: first, by its making visible the figure of the excluded – the stateless, and racial and sexual outsider – upon the rarified set of the showpieces of national spectacle; and second, by directing the power of film to resist conventional representational systems, by producing an experience of perceptual creativity that denies the certainty of identity and the clarity of signs on which hegemonic order rests. In this regard, *Giardini*'s evocative realm of perceptual contingency might be seen to risk a certain aestheticization, which attends the film's hyper-sensitive visual immediacy, no doubt intensified by the saturation that results from its basis in 35mm stock and the expansiveness of its panoramic aspect. A radical impressionism ensues at times, exemplified by the camera's prolonged dwelling

---

3. Sands and other IRA members were struggling to gain 'prisoner of war' status for Republicans found guilty by the British of violent opposition to British rule (which the IRA claimed to be legitimate resistance). I have written on McQueen's films at length in "The Art of Darkness: on Steve McQueen," *October*, no.114 (Fall 2005), pp.61-89; and "Moving Images of Globalization," *Grey Room 37* (forthcoming, 2009).

on radiant flower petals and its close-up depictions of the colourful splendour of beetles and the earthy camouflage of a garden spider. Such privileging of stylistic concerns also appears in the film-noir associations of the film's frequent images shot in nocturnal environments, as stages for shady dealings and suspenseful visions without obvious critique or clear subversive point.

Yet this aestheticization is not a matter of beauty for beauty's sake; rather, it concerns the beauty implicit in the political revelation of order's contingency, realised by drawing the viewer's eye to the out-of-frame and to the in-between, in other words, the non-spectacular and unscripted happenings of life outside dominant political order. Politics, according to political theorist Chantal Mouffe, requires the presence of two concepts: hegemony and antagonism.[4] Hegemony, the maintenance of rule so that order appears natural, seeks to neutralise the antagonism that reveals reality as contingent, as open to change. In the context of *Giardini*, however, it is the natural order that is portrayed as fiction, as when the blurred movements of greyhounds interlope like wraiths among the living. Beauty here is the power of the image that focuses desire upon, and draws attention to life outside the dominance of

order (national, imperial, normative, sexual, perceptual), doing so by inventing its conceivable existence in a context where art has historically sung the glory of the nation state. In *Giardini*, beauty arises in the imagination of life beyond and outside the conventional orders of art and politics.

That this order of nationality – established with the first Biennale of 1895, which continued the tradition of imperial international expositions of the mid-nineteenth century – is not in fact timeless, is of course nothing new, and will not be revelatory to many. The revelation in *Giardini* concerns, rather, the experience of a film that generates the space of contingency so powerfully in its experiential register, wherein the possibility of survival outside of conventional orders may transform from the virtual dimension of the image into realisation elsewhere.

---

4. See Chantal Mouffe, *On the Political* (London: Routledge, 2005).

The film GIARDINI has been produced
with funding from
Marian Goodman Gallery, New York and Paris

outset.

Outset Contemporary Art Fund

The Art Fund charity, London

In collaboration with Thomas Dane Gallery, London

With assistance from the British Council

Producer: Pinky Ghundale
Director of photography: Sean Bobbitt
Focus puller: Gordon Segrove
Camera assistant: Tash Gamper
Sound recordist: Andy Paddon
Editor: Jessica de Koning
Sound mix: Marco Vermaas
Post production: Filmdoc, Deluxe London, Framestore

Service company in Venice: CRG International
Director: Rosanna Roditi
Production manager: Fabrizio Weis
Assistant manager: Niccolò Salavato
Assistant director: Gianluca Caponegro
Production assistant: Alvise Facchinetti
Art department: Marino Ingrassia
Art department: Luca Masarotto
Video assist operator: Maurizio Cesana
Runner: Jury Basiato and Chiara Sambo
Production secretary: Roger Roditi
Casting: Daniela Foà

British Pavilion manager and location liaison:
Luisa Trabucchi

ACKNOWLEDGEMENTS

Giorgio Basile, Ignazio Cortivo, Paolo Franciosi, Moulaye Niang,
Umberto Meneghetti, Edoardo Veneziano, Marouane Zotti

Cani Attori and EuropeanGreyhound Network:
Salvio Annunziato,
Loredana Adoretti, Giovanni Bruzzichelli,
Renato Corna, Chiara Ertolla,
Matteo Meloni, Paolo Panizzari

With thanks for the cooperation of
the Venice Film Commission

Special thanks to:
Martine d'Anglejan-Chatillon for
Thomas Dane Gallery, London
Marian Goodman and Rose Lord for
Marian Goodman Gallery, New York and Paris

Commissioner for the British Pavilion: Andrea Rose
Curator: Richard Riley
Exhibition coordinator: Sarah Gillett
Exhibition assistant: Gemma Latty
Technical manager: Marcus Alexander
Technical team: Matt Arthurs, Tony Connor, Julian Hodges
Visual Arts registrar: Silvia Bordin
Events manager: Nansi O'Connor
British Council press officer: Eleanor Hutchins
PR consultant: Calum Sutton

Installation designer: Sue MacDiarmid

British Pavilion manager: Luisa Trabucchi

Director British Council Italy: Paul Docherty
Arts Assistant British Council Italy: Marina Machelli

The British Council would like to thank
Thomas Dane and Martine d'Anglejan-Chatillon
of Thomas Dane Gallery, London
Marian Goodman, Rose Lord and Agnès Fierobe
of Marian Goodman Gallery, New York and Paris

ACKNOWLEDGEMENTS
Philip Abraham, Phil Allison, Keith Davey, Francesco Donadio,
Julian Eguiguren, Nick Gunner, Tom Haines, Tim Harvey,
Kate Jazwinski, Catherine Jay, Anthony Makinson, Piero Morello,
Roxanna Pennie, Amy Pettifer, Leigh Robb, Roberto Rosolen,
Hannah Schlotter, Louise Taylor

VENICE BIENNALE SELECTION COMMITTEE
Martin Barlow, Director Oriel Mostyn, Llandudno
Katrina Brown, Director The Common Guild, Glasgow
Penelope Curtis, Curator Henry Moore Institute, Leeds
Stephen Deuchar, Director Tate Britain, London
Alex Farquharson, Director Centre for Contemporary Art, Nottingham
Jack Persekian, Director Al Ma'mal Foundation, East Jerusalem
Declan McGonagle, Chair in Art & Design & Director School of Art and Design, University of Ulster, Belfast
Magdalene Odundo, Professor of Ceramics, University College of the Creative Arts, Farnham
Richard Riley, Head of Exhibitions, British Council, London
Adrian Searle, Chief Critic, *The Guardian*, London
Chair: Andrea Rose, Director of Visual Arts, British Council, London

la Biennale di Venezia

53. Esposizione
Internazionale
d'Arte

Partecipazioni nazionali

Published by the British Council
10 Spring Gardens, London SW1A 2BN
on the occasion of the exhibition
STEVE McQUEEN GIARDINI
British Pavilion, 53rd Venice Biennale
7 June – 22 November 2009

© British Council 2009

ISBN 978-086355-625-8

Photographs by Sean Bobbitt
© Steve McQueen 2009

Text © T.J. Demos 2009

Edited by Richard Riley

Designed by Richard Hollis
Assistant: Ana Estrougo

Printed in the United Kingdom
by Butler Tanner and Dennis,
Frome

This book
is dedicated to
LUISA TRABUCCHI
in her last year as
British Pavilion Manager